Saving Fruit

Lynda Plater

Monday, February 1908

In the watery house,
a lean-to with
white-washed walls,
a grate beneath the copper
and a pump with a
swan's neck handle,
is where Great-grandma
washed white sheets
while they were
little but threads
held by hand-stitched hems.
Grated soap
tide-marked the tub.

Wringing out water
made the skin
of her hands flayed.
Muscles ached
with mangle turn.
The clothes-line drawn down
sagged with the weight
of sodden linen
which dripped down
the nape of her neck.

Great-grandad at the cockle bed, 1910

He is the line of sea,
drawing in rills and runs
of tide as he rakes cockles.
A North Sea, salt-filled,
loose-limbed and watery
in his work rattling shells
as waves do at a sand shelf.
Their ebb and flow
is a roll, a gathering.

His horse, sleep-filled,
sandfly tired, utters snorts.
Cart loaded, sacks
draining their brine
on wood. It is
a steady pace home –
a horse which can find
its own way round
butt runs and soft sand.

At the yard, enamel buckets
rattle as man
and wife rinse shells:
he on pump, she with
water rills up her arms.
They are both singing.

Midsummer harvest, 1911

Thin ring of time
posed for the photographer
who counts for light
to release them –
catch of hair wisp,
cotton collar fray,
chapped hands
from plaiting onions.
Great-grandma sits
with the infant in her lap;
husband and eldest son
each side.
Their hands hold
the cobs of twine.

Onions sway,
unseen, pendular,
drying in draughts
from the shed roof beam.

Great-grandma preserves fruit, 1912

October forewarns a February hunger.
Equipoise of fruit on her palm:
a fleshy claim to glass jars
where plums are sugared,
purpling towards winter.

The pantry's white-washed walls
bloom a harvest of preserve in lines:
brings liquor to my tongue to have
her dialect of slow marsh vowels
dissolved in mine.

Samphire, August 1913.

In the wide-brimmed hat
Mrs Lewis wove from
July's straw stalks left
from the hot year's yield,
Great-grandma gathers samphire
at the sea field,
                            its fat flesh
lifted to her basket.
When a plover rose
and twined the sky
she sucked green stems,
let salt and seaweed
salve her tongue.

Insomnia, 1915

Fleeting, his synapses
quiver on his son
somewhere
in another land.

Great-grandad is lost
in inked night.
Hears fox snort
round walls.
It has come
on its trail
from shoreline
where its lair
gapes dark.

Then Lucy,
thin-breathed
in the bed
makes a cold,
damp spot
at his neck.
In and out.
In and out.
A heart worn.

On watch, 1916

Stars scrawled to the border
with wire strewn to posts
and bits of sheeps' fleece
caught like white flags.

When Joe came they lit fags,
made red glows
in their own firmament
among sand and sandbags.

A distant thud from the west
but Sid and Joe talked
as if they were on the corner
of Stortford Street

and there was Mrs Hibberd
gossiping with Joe's Mam
and Sid said he could
just eat fish and chips

from the corner shop.
They stubbed tab ends in dust
and Joe rubbed cold knuckles.
Sid said *That's the trouble*

with you townies,
you can't stand cold!
and then they laughed.
And in the west another thud.

Sid's last battle, 23^d September 1918

Nazareth weary.
A fight with Turks
in the streets.
Horses now fettered,
clumsy in fear.
Prisoners kneel
or sit on heels.
Some lie sleeping
on their sides.

Sid thinks of September,
the loose ends of beans
swaying on poles.
Dad digs them in.
Mam gathering seeds
from the borders.
Little brother at his book,
drawing sycamore seeds:
their light wings held
with a promise to spin.
Spinning.
Spinning on the wind.

Sid's first days of leaving Palestine, 1919

Soldiers abandoned
their oral history.
Stood port-side
until Haifa receded
into the sea.
A choppy sailing
brought the men
seasickness and horses
kicking in the hold.
At Southampton
they left their kit,
starred out
in all directions home.

His mother flung
wet arms round him.
Little brother nudged in.
Dad said
Now then, lad
and lit his pipe.
But Sid's words
wouldn't come:
not in the yard, or stable
where the horse slept,
not in the winter lane
nor at the shore
where waves rolled in
with black seal heads
bobbing dark full-stops
inside the foam.
Palestine
would not
submerge
but remained
tiding in him.

Great-grandma's still life, 1921

Four oranges
in a blue dish
under the window.
So exotic!
Yet hard to eat –
bitter on lips,
juice stinging
fingers' winter cuts.
And oh, those pips!

Shade around them,
midnight blue
where fruit touched
until she lit lamps –
brought men in
from the frosted field.
And after bread
and cheese
they all sat,
watched fragrant
fruit aglow.

She wondered
about still life,
finding the palette
of the fruit.
Easier still,
she thought,
are calyces,
those hard
dried sepals
where once
blossom dwelt
now a history –

an unknown hand
which reached,
turned the fruit,
drew it from its stem.

End of a living, 1931

He will no longer be heard
calling from Eastgate
as women wait with cups
for a gill of cockles
raked from Donna Nook.
His green cart (painted
with his name in cream)
already begins to flake.
The horse which drew it
has dropped amid the clatter
of buckets on to straw,
now lies with heart stalled.
One eye up.

The old man kneels,
his hands amid the greasy mane.
The last suck of air, then
a hessian sack drawn
over that one dull eye.

Great-grandma has come –
leads her man home
through the yard
where numb stars
wash about his dark.

Saving fruit

And here the fingers are in the ruffle
of newspaper around the blush and
smooth skin of apples being laid out

for a later fruiting, gathering juice
as they sleep. Let us lie down then
on the bed of words in long night

as great-grandmother did and spoke
soft to her man as he roused sheets
to lie beside her in the feather bed

using the soft pronoun *thou*
as address. Not archaic but tender
as the blueness at the window

where the moon hangs. She lays
cold feet on his thick calves and
he murmurs *Thou art cold, lass*

with his whole roundness turning
to her thin frame all gentler
than the *you* we use. Thus,

lying like fruit, untightened, their
vocabulary for apples is thinned
leaving windfall words unsaid.

Laboured hands, 1951

I

In the presence of slow hours
he cuts greens on frosted field

until his fingers weep,
stain the long-bladed knife,

and take away the feel
of sacks of greens

tied up with binder-band
and lined up at field's edge.

II

She wields a mighty frown
as he comes in, sees he can

no longer hold cutlery;
has to palm the cup.

She washes the cuts,
poultices the fingers

in a swelter of blanched
comfrey leaves and dock.

III

In sleep his hands
are wound in tight,

sweating and sore within
torn sheet strips.

With dawn he unwinds
the remedy of cloth, peels

off the comfrey compress.
Fields are white with hoar-frost.

Turning

He was with gulls
in the follow of the plough
in its departing
up the long field.
The earth was turning,
a curling of an autumn
into winter.
And the man felt
he too was moving
to another season
with furrows fumbling
at his feet
and eye unsure
of clear cut lines.

The tractor turned
in a long landscape
and flakes of gulls
turned with it.
The old man watched,
felt its coming,
knife-edged furrows
meeting in the gather
of earth for fallow.
And on its passing
he was with gulls
between their flight;
saw the ploughshare
steeling straight.

Mam makes bread

In the waft of flour
rising above the bowl,
her arms and hands
are dusty with promise.
Yeast froth, sugared
in a cup, is poured
in the flour well.
Warm water added.
Stirred. Then sides
of the bowl cleared
of the mix by
the palette of her hand.
Dough. Ruffled
on the board
and knuckled in.
Every so often
the glance
of her wedding ring.

Lipstick

On the sideboard,
red lipstick
in a gold-tone case
of vintage Arden
has the smell
of Mam when
she bent low
to kiss me.
It has the colour
of Auntie Ruth's
roseate lips
which held,
one moment,
a trembling
crumb of cake,
and grandma's
lip print
on a china cup.
And it holds
sweet oil taste
on my novice lip
as my sister
first painted it –
her lips stretched
to mirror mine.

The ring ouzel, November 2018

The boundary hedge
has hawthorn boughs
thick as a man's arm
to uplift blackthorn,
beech, elder, ash,
since Grandad layered it
with Sunboy Lamming
in the winter of '49.
A cold, sharp work
of many days
weaving wood
and willow wand.

In their weft of twigs
the ring ouzel has come.
It is late, a leafless season,
and poor place for seed
and berry: scant pickings
for a sea-wing home.

Small bird, sloe-grey eyed,
a white collar like a pastor,
watchful in the space
of summer into autumn:
a migration held
one moment
in its quivered wing.

Sailing lesson

Just then our wherry's white wing
turned us on the water
so we were among reeds which hished
and swayed away from the hull
until we were with a heron, stark
and startled by our closeness,
the eddy lapping at his grey legs.
A dark eye stared at us, mocked
our lack of skill with boats until
his prowess in sails prevailed –
he widened, pushed down air, rose –
sounding not a song but a crawk
which made the whole keel shake.

Jar of clay

But we have this treasure in earthen vessels,
that the excellency of the power may be of God,
and not of us. (2 Corinthians 4:7)

In mudflats
curlew bills reflect
a sloped world
before sun comes up.
They break
soft molluscs
in rising light.
Their legs part
soft skin of pools

as potter's fingers
in slip, draw
up a bowl,
leave it unglazed
to hold earths' mould.

She has put in
sanderling –
clipped them in clay,
their wings
in multitude.
And around the rim
the bittern, secret
of reeds, hidden
in a soft scrape.

Rooks in winter

They have spilled their inkwell with wide wing
to dribble black down winter trees, into
untidy sticks of last spring's nests.

They make an etch of marsh in December
with their span on papered sky – border
the flat land and a few wet reeds

and all the while their scraped cawing
moves their air around and down
to watchers who have come,

brought upturned faces held in muffling
wools and hoods to see the quire
of seasoned patterns in the air.

The viewers are silent in their gather, shuffle
cold feet in boots which have wet earth
and leaf-mould in deep treads.

Gather

Now fields are ploughed
in lines of brown corduroy
apart from end-rows
where the blade has turned
a shoulder and where
blackthorn, threadbare
after October storms
leaves just a twine
of sloes like tiny buttons
on the boughs, so
we have set out
in the mercy of a dry hour
to the edge of Pinder's Field
where watercourses meet.
We have come for
the murmuration.
Outcrops of starlings
from Pye's Hall and
the Brickpit Pond
come in and ravel up:
ten thousand wings frayed
in flight give breath to sky,
fill air with chattering bills
in a vocabulary of mystery.

Then, as they began,
they fold into the cloth of dusk,
its soil and reed, its hedgerow.
As we walk home
our sleeves and shoulders brush.

Family

Great-grandad – George "Ratty" Cook (Approx dates 1858-1942)
Cockler and market gardener

Great-grandma – Mary "Lucy" Cook (1871-1961)
Housewife and mother

Grandad – Albert Sidney "Sid" Cook (1895-1951)
Son of Lucy and Ratty. Market gardener.
Lincolnshire Yeomanry in Egypt and Palestine. 1915-18

Little brother – George Henry "Georgie" Cook (1911-68)
Only other surviving child of Lucy and "Ratty"

Mam – Edith Mary Macdonald (nee Cook) (1923-1971)
Only surviving child of Sid and Nellie Cook

Acknowledgements:
'Turning' was previously published in *Lines Review.*
'Saving Fruit' was published in the pamphlet
Three Seasons for Burning (Wayleave 2015)

Cover image: 'Apple' watercolour, 1990 Lynda Plater

published by
Wayleave,
8 Buoymasters,
St George's Quay,
Lancaster,
LA1 1HL
www.wayleavepress.co.uk

Printed by
Andrews, Main Street, Bentham, LA2 7HQ